Learning to Read, Step by Step!

Ready to Read   **Preschool–Kindergarten**
• big type and easy words • rhyme and rhythm • picture clues
For children who know the alphabet and are eager to
begin reading.

Reading with Help   **Preschool–Grade 1**
• basic vocabulary • short sentences • simple stories
For children who recognize familiar words and sound out
new words with help.

Reading on Your Own   **Grades 1–3**
• engaging characters • easy-to-follow plots • popular topics
For children who are ready to read on their own.

Reading Paragraphs   **Grades 2–3**
• challenging vocabulary • short paragraphs • exciting stories
For newly independent readers who read simple sentences
with confidence.

Ready for Chapters   **Grades 2–4**
• chapters • longer paragraphs • full-color art
For children who want to take the plunge into chapter books
but still like colorful pictures.

STEP INTO READING® is designed to give every child a successful
reading experience. The grade levels are only guides; children will progress
through the steps at their own speed, developing confidence in their reading.
The F&P Text Level on the back cover serves as another tool to help you
choose the right book for your child.

Remember, a lifetime love of reading starts with a single step!

For Heidi Kilgras, with many thanks
—M.K.

For my cousin, Harry. Beyond the sky.
—G.B.

Text copyright © 2016 by Monica Kulling
Cover art and interior illustrations copyright © 2016 by Gene Barretta

Visit us on the Web!
StepIntoReading.com
randomhousekids.com

Educators and librarians, for a variety of teaching tools, visit us at RHTeachersLibrarians.com

Library of Congress Cataloging-in-Publication Data
Names: Kulling, Monica, author. | Barretta, Gene, illustrator.
Title: Sky high: George Ferris's big wheel / by Monica Kulling; illustrated by Gene Barretta.
Other titles: Step into reading. Step 3 book.
Description: New York: Random House, [2016] | Series: Step into reading. Step 3
Identifiers: LCCN 2015038771 | ISBN 978-1-101-93452-4 (trade pbk.) |
ISBN 978-1-101-93453-1 (hardcover library binding) | ISBN 978-1-101-93454-8 (ebook)
Subjects: LCSH: Ferris, George Washington Gale, 1859–1896—Juvenile literature. |
Inventors—United States—Biography—Juvenile literature. |
Structural engineering—United States—Biography—Juvenile literature. |
Ferris wheels—History—Juvenile literature.
Classification: LCC TA140.F455 K85 2016 | DDC 624.1092—dc23

Printed in the United States of America

10 9 8 7 6 5 4 3 2 1

This book has been officially leveled by using the F&P Text Level Gradient™ Leveling System.

Sky High

George Ferris's Big Wheel

by Monica Kulling

illustrated by Gene Barretta

Random House 🏠 New York

George loved to watch
the big waterwheel
go round and round.
It scooped up river water
for people and animals to drink.
It watered fields.
It ground corn into meal.
George loved the sound
of the turning wheel.

It was 1867.

George Washington Gale Ferris Jr.

lived on a ranch in Nevada.

George rode horses.

The waterwheel

on the Carson River turned

through winter and spring,

summer and fall.

As the wheel turned,

George grew taller and taller.

He did chores.

And the waterwheel turned.

George left home
to go to school
at age fourteen.
When he graduated
from college,
he was ready
to work as an engineer.
He would design
bridges and roads,
canals and dams.

George moved to Pittsburgh,
Pennsylvania.
He got his dream job.
He was asked
to design a bridge
across the Allegheny River.

George often brought
his dog, Sal, along
to watch the workers
building "his" bridge.

George married Margaret in 1886.

He started his own business.

Men put up the sign:

G.W.G. Ferris & Company.

"It's a humdinger," said George.

Margaret agreed.

"Woof!" barked Sal.

She liked it too!

It was 1892.

A World's Fair was coming

to Chicago in 1893!

Engineers wanted to build

something eye-catching

like Paris's Eiffel Tower.

Margaret read about it

in the papers.

"There's a competition," she said.

"You must enter."

Margaret packed George's bag.

He took a train to Chicago

to meet with other engineers.

Daniel Burnham was in charge of
the fair's buildings.

Everyone wanted to build a tower.

"We're not copying Paris," he said.

George sat quietly in a corner,
doodling on a napkin.

Mr. Burnham looked at the doodle.

"People would ride on the wheel,"

said George.

"They would have

a bird's-eye view of the fair

and of Lake Michigan."

"It won't work!" said Mr. Burnham.

"It's a crazy idea!"

shouted others.

Mr. Burnham rejected
George's drawings three times!
"Winds will tear your wheel
to pieces," he said.
"People will fall to the ground!
Think up another idea."

But time was running out
and no one had a better idea.
In December,
Mr. Burnham agreed
to let George build his wheel.
But he would have to pay
for it himself!
And it had to be ready
on opening day,
May 1, 1893.
Could George do it?

DE

MARCH

BRUARY

1 2 3

1 2 3 4

8 9 10

5 6 7

6 7 8 9 10 11

5 6 7 8 9 10

13 14 15 16 17

None of the banks in town
would lend George money.
They laughed him out the door.
They had never heard
of such a crazy idea.

George's friends helped.

They found rich men

who were willing to give him

the $400,000 he needed.

Now the work could begin.

When George wanted
to call the ride
the Monster Wheel,
no one would let him.
It was called the Ferris Wheel.

Digging began in January.

It was one of

the worst winters on record.

Workers had to use dynamite

to blast the frozen ground.

Eight holes were dug
to pour in concrete
for the base.
It had to hold the weight
of two million pounds!

George built train tracks
so that a freight train
could haul the wheel's parts
to the building site.

The center—or axle—
weighed seventy tons!
It was the largest piece of steel
ever forged in America.

The wheel was built

one pie-shaped section at a time.

The day came when

the last piece

was hoisted up.

Would it fit?

George hoped his math was correct.

It was!

The piece fit.

The fair had already begun,
but the wheel wasn't ready.
Thirty-six steel cars
still had to be put on.
Each car would hold
sixty passengers.

On June 21,

a crowd gathered

at the Ferris Wheel.

George made a speech.

He blew a whistle.

Tweet!

It was time for the first ride.

The fair had already begun,
but the wheel wasn't ready.
Thirty-six steel cars
still had to be put on.
Each car would hold
sixty passengers.

On June 10,
the crew began
to hang the cars.
When the job was done,
the wheel looked like
the waterwheel
George had loved
as a boy.

On June 21,

a crowd gathered

at the Ferris Wheel.

George made a speech.

He blew a whistle.

Tweet!

It was time for the first ride.

George, Margaret, and Sal

got into a steel car.

So did the mayor of Chicago.

A forty-piece orchestra

came along for the ride!

Slowly,

the big wheel turned.

The wheel went round
and stopped at the top.
They could see for miles!
Margaret toasted George.
The orchestra played
"America the Beautiful."
Then, slowly,
the wheel started again.

George's wheel
was 264 feet tall.
Today many Ferris Wheels
are much taller.

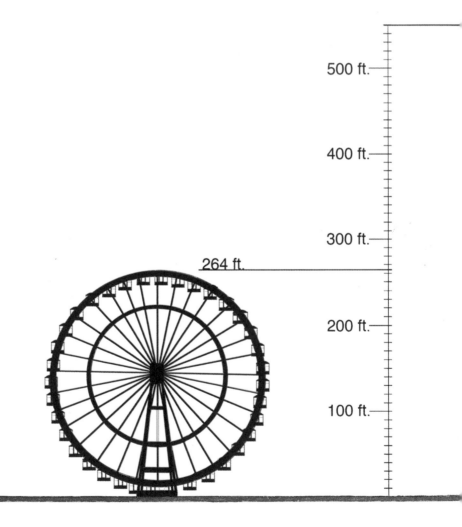

500 ft.—

400 ft.—

300 ft.—

264 ft.

200 ft.—

100 ft.—

The High Roller,

in Las Vegas,

is more than twice as tall

as George's big wheel.

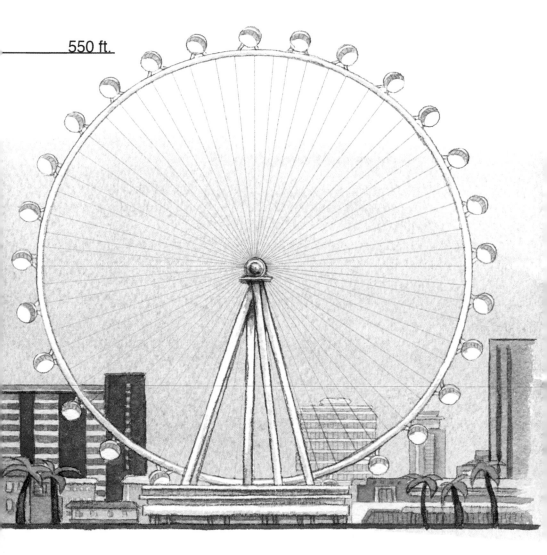

550 ft.

In 2015,

New York City began to build

the country's biggest wheel,

designed to be nearly

630 feet tall.

The view should be amazing.

Just as it was from

George Ferris's first wheel.